HOW TO GIVE A
MIND-BLOWING
BJ

THIS IS A CARLTON BOOK

Text and design copyright © Carlton Books Limited 2007

First published in 2007

This edition reprinted 2013 by
Carlton Books Limited
20 Mortimer Street
London W1T 3JW

A CIP catalogue record for this book is available from the British Library.

UK ISBN 978 1 84442 072 8
US ISBN 978 1 84732 014 8

Printed and bound in China

Executive Editor: Lisa Dyer
Senior Art Editor: Gülen Shevki-Taylor
Design: Tim Pattinson
Production Controller: Fifi von Trapp

HOW TO GIVE A
MIND-BLOWING
BJ

LISA SUSSMAN

CARLTON
BOOKS

Section One

Oral Studies

It's a no-brainer to say that men are suckers for blowjobs. According to *The Hite Report*, almost all the 7,000+ men polled listed fellatio as their hands-down most beloved sexual past-time. Which is why it's unfortunate many women don't have the first idea how to handle his favourite tool. They grab, fumble and give up. But here's a little secret: The reason he rates blowjobs so highly is because to him your mouth feels like your vagina with a brain. So read on for your below-the-belt guide to giving him some smart lip service.

Have you ever seen a grown man melt?
You will.

Director's Cut

One thing – depending on where his penis hails from, he may still be wearing a turtleneck (America is one of the few countries where the men are circumcised for non-religious reasons). The foreskin (a loose fold of skin that covers the glans or the head of the penis) doesn't always stretch back and allow full access once he's erect, so check out the uncut version of the tip for getting under his hood.

Basic Bobs

Tongue-whipping his penis into a frenzy isn't complicated. Follow these basic seven steps blow-by-blow for mind-searing oral sex he'll love to get and you'll love to give. Remember, practice makes perfect.

1

Lose the fear. The average guy's equipment is a manageable 3½ in (8.6 cm) turned off and 5½ in (13.7 cm) turned on.

2

A little enthusiasm goes a looong way. More than an incredible body or a great technique, what gets him going is knowing that you truly want his penis in your mouth. So before you even get near his fly, let him know how thrilled you are to get on kissing terms with his little guy and not just doing charity work ("Please, please can I go down on you?"). Contrary to urban legend, most men take longer than a boiled egg to get off. Expect to spend at least ten minutes down there.

3

Take care removing the merchandise. Most zipper injuries (just reading these words will make many men cringe) occur on the un-zip when less attention is being paid. (Extra goddess points for unzipping him with your mouth.)

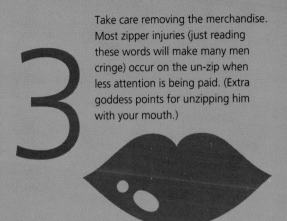

However you arrange yourselves, never force a good penis down once he's up. Putting downward pressure on an erect penis strains the suspensory ligaments, the two long tendons that give him the wherewithal to become stiff in the first place. Stretched too far, they'll lose their spring which will result in an erection that may permanently point down instead of up. The key is to strike a pose that has him moving upward into your mouth. Read on for a slant on the top four pole positions you can take.

- **Call Girl:** One of the most popular, he stands up or kneels and you crouch between his legs with your head at the level of his crotch.
  Ups: You get plenty of freedom of movement to show off your stuff.
  Downs: He can control the thrust and depth. Put your hand at base to stay in the driver's seat.

  - **69:** This is a great position where you can both give and receive at the same time by lying down facing each other with your heads at opposite ends (variations on the theme: he's on top and you're on bottom, vice versa or you lie side by side).
    Ups: You get as good you give.
    Downs: Since you're both caught up in your own blissfest, you never get or give all that much. Much better is to do a 6/9 where you take turns taking care of each other.

- **Lying Down, Part One:** He's flat on his back and you're kneeling over him.
  Ups: You are in total control.
  Downs: None, actually.

- **Lying Down, Part Two:** You're flat on your back and he's ducking and diving over you.
Ups: He gets plenty of feel-good depth.
Downs: He gets plenty of feel-good depth. Try lying with your head slightly hanging over the edge of bed. While he essentially stays in control of the thrusting, your throat will now be opened wide enough to be able to take him in without gagging (plus it looks porn-star sexy).

- **Sitting:** He lounges on a chair or sofa with you next to him, bent over his bounty.
Ups: This is a good position for a relative beginner as the limited range of movement means he can't thrust up into your mouth.
Downs: You can't take that much in your mouth once you become more adept. Change positions so that you're kneeling between his legs instead of bowing over them.

5

Cover
your teeth
with your lips.
The odd nip here and
there is fine, but he doesn't
want you to treat his delicate tool like
an ear of corn. Along the same lines, don't
play rough (unless he asks for it). Yanking back
the foreskin, sucking too hard, pumping up and
down like you're trying to draw water from
a dry well and snagging any part of it on
jewellery (including mouth studs) are
all no-no's.

Start
slobbering. The
wetter things are down
there, the better. Always have
some water nearby in case you get
cottonmouth (check out tips 33
to 38 for more on keeping
things juicy).

6

7

Squeeze the shaft of his joystick with one hand to keep him steady and slide your (very) wet mouth over it until your lips meet your hand. That's it. Don't suck – or blow, for that matter. What you (and he) want to start with is a slow up-and-down movement that rubs against the sensitive skin of his penis.

Uncut Version: Don't take him out to play just yet. Instead, moisten the area around the foreskin; then gently edge your tongue under the hood and swirl it around before sliding it down. You can then either hold it down at the base of the shaft or pump it up and down the shaft. BTW, his penis is not a microphone. So don't speak into it and ask how you are doing. If he is enjoying himself, his moans will give it away.

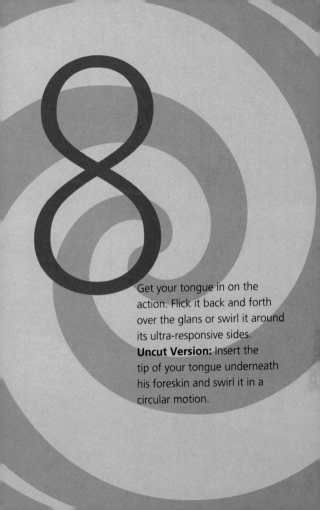

Get your tongue in on the action. Flick it back and forth over the glans or swirl it around its ultra-responsive sides. **Uncut Version:** Insert the tip of your tongue underneath his foreskin and swirl it in a circular motion.

9

Keep in rhythm.
Start off slowly so
every movement is
exquisite torture;
only pick up the
pace as he gets
ready to explode.

Get monotonous.
Though your mouth
may feel as if it's about
to fall off, keep steady
and keep on suckin'.
While lots of variety is
good at the beginning,
don't change your mouth
moves once you get him
to the edge or you may
have to start all over from
scratch (see tips 69 to 71
for more on giving him
a blow-out finish).

10

Cold Start

Don't worry if he's as flabby as an old lady's triceps when you start your play. You'll his penis into a hard body lickety split with these buff moves. One word of caution before you begin: Wait until he's fully ready to play before starting the heavy tackles. If he thrusts his penis before it is fully erect, he risks bending and buckling injuries, which could end up benching him for the season at best and possibly leaving him with a painfully perpetual bend when he gets erect.

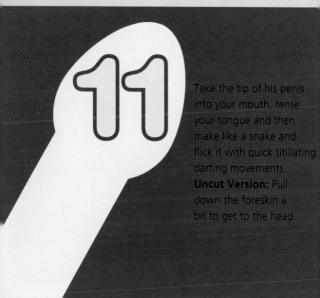

Take the tip of his penis into your mouth, tense your tongue and then make like a snake and flick it with quick titillating darting movements. **Uncut Version:** Pull down the foreskin a bit to get to the head.

Warm him up with this simple move.
First, gently take him into your mouth
to get him wet from head to base and
then dry him off by gently blowing
your hot breath over the entire area.

12

Take your time. A series of pit stops that tickle and tease will have him springing to attention before you even get near his cylinder. Kiss and lick around his inner thighs, his testicles and then slowly up his shaft toward the gland. Once there, tickle the area with your tongue until he's in high gear.

Come Up For Air

Beginners at fellatio tend to hold their breath. But you don't want to pass out before he does. Here's how to breathe without disrupting the action.

14

Whatever his size of tool, you'll be able to take it in your mouth if you exhale before you take the plunge. Here's how it works: When you inhale and then hold your breath, your throat becomes like an inflated balloon, pushing your tongue and the back of your mouth higher. But when you exhale and then hold your breath, the vacuum in your trachea pulls the back of your throat lower, adding up to 2 in (5 cm) to your capacity.

15

Try breathing through your nose.

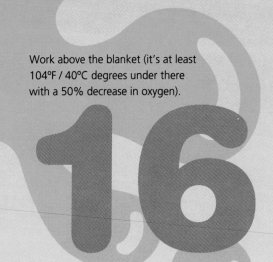

Work above the blanket (it's at least
104°F / 40°C degrees under there
with a 50% decrease in oxygen).

16

Mouth Drills

If you've been doing sit-ups and lunges in order to impress your loverboy, you've been working the wrong muscles. Instead, try some simple stretching exercises to keep your tongue and sucking muscles limber and strong. Repeat each of the following exercises ten times.

- **Go Fish:** Push your lips all the way forward, rolling the insides out and then opening and closing your mouth much like a guppy.

- **Spin the Bottle:** Tie a string around the neck of a half-filled large bottle of water and lift it using just your lips.

- **Air Lip:** With your mouth firmly closed, push the air upward so that your upper lip blows out. Hold for three seconds, then release.

- **Tongue Yoga:** Stretch your tongue out as far as it will go and try to touch first your nose, and then your chin.

- **Lip Wagger:** Circle your tongue around your lips in a clockwise motion and then reverse the motion to counter-clockwise.

- **Buy a Body Double:** Get a double-decker ice-cream cone and slowly lick all around it. Then put the whole mound of ice cream in your mouth. When it starts to drip down the side of the cone, use your tongue to catch the drops.

18

Sexpert-approved tricks to prevent mid-action injury.

- Go "up" on him instead. Kneel on the floor so that his head and shoulders rest on the floor or bed, his back angles toward your stomach and chest and his bottom rests at your neck level. Then wrap your arms right below his hips to support him. You'll seem strong as a weightlifter, but it's gravity that's really doing all the lifting.

- Strategize. The more you prepare the field before you tackle his tackle, the less time you'll need to spend in an oral scrum-down. So go offside and work him up with some clever hand moves (see Section Two: Tickle His Pickle for ideas). When he's about to score, up the action with some easy oral plays. Run your tongue up and down his shaft to lubricate him, use the tip of your tongue to trace a trail around the base of his penis or gently suck on his balls as you move your hand up and down his shaft, kiss your way along his member, flick your tongue against the nerve-packed fraenulum (that little ridge on the underside where the head meets the shaft). At the last moment, take him fully in your mouth.

- If your jaw gets tired mid-action, switch to licking and kissing his penis and/or stimulating it manually.

- Use a chin rest. Put one pillow beneath his hips and another under your chest. His lower back will be more relaxed, and it'll be easier for him to adjust his knees and legs, allowing for more sensation. Prop your chin on your fist, with your pinkie down, and use a finger to put pressure on his perineum (the magic bit of flesh between his balls and bottom). Watch him hit the roof.

Getting Into Shape

Sighs do matter so match your mouth play
to his penis shape and size.

Monster Dick: If he's on the large
size, don't be heroic and try to choke up all
of him at once. You'll just end up spitting him
right out again. To stop him from rear-ending your
tonsils, have him lie on his back as you crouch over
his crotch. That way you can pull back if he pushes in
too deep. Best of all, you'll leave your hands free so you
can use them on the boys. As he grows to full size, lick
the length of his penis, alternating between sweeping
up-and-down strokes and circular motions. When
you're ready to take more of him into your mouth,
try this gag-proof technique: Lick or lube your hands
(study tips 34 to 38 for which lubes to use). Then form
a tube with one hand and put it against your lips. Wrap
your mouth around his shaft and slide your mouth
and hand up and down in unison.

Uncut Version: When his appendage is on the XL size,
his extra layer of skin may not retract completely. If you
want more of him to work with, gently push it toward
the base of his shaft.

Short Dick: If he comes in a mini, make the most of what he's got by taking the whole thing into your mouth and sucking hard. The tight fit will make him feel like he's driving a stretch limo.

Uncut Version: Make him feel like the biggest man in the room by holding one hand in an L position firmly at the base of his penis, pulling the skin back from the base (in the direction of his pelvis). Not only does it make him look bigger, but it also heightens sensitivity. You may have to peel back the loose folds of skin to get at his good stuff.

20

21

Fat Dick: Yes, it's sweet when you can gobble up his entire sausage. But it isn't really necessary to stuff yourself. Since the most sensitive part of his equipment is in the first 1½ in (3.8 cm), you can still give him a tongue lashing by concentrating your energies there. Swirl your tongue around the ridge where the head meets the shaft; then gently suck the tip.

Uncut Version: Beware of bunching. You can flatten any lumpy bits with a light push of your hand.

Section Two

Tickle His Pickle

Employ backup. Don't make the mistake
of thinking oral sex is like soccer in that
the use of hands is not permitted.
If you only use your mouth, you risk dishing out
the world's longest blowjob. Not because your
mouthwork isn't seductive and steamy, but because
most men enjoy (and often need) extra stimulation
to intensify and speed up their joyride to bliss.
Master these multitasking tips and he'll love you
for your carnal coordination.

Get A Grip

Start with the basics – here, six steps to perfecting your handshake.

Which hand do you write with? Then make sure that paw has easy access when you deliver the goods or you may end up with worker's cramp (with no guaranteed compensation).

Lick your hand. Unlike women, men don't have built-in lubricants. If you use your new extra-strong grip on him dry, you'll probably give him carpet burn (tips 33 to 38 will whet your appetite with more ideas on how to juice him up).

24

To perform a workaday, no-frills handjob (which will still plaster a goofy grin on his face), firmly but gently grasp your hand around the base of the penis and slide it upward until it reaches the head. Then rub your palm over the head in tiny exquisite circles. Slide your hand back down to base camp and, adjusting your hand so your palm is squeezing the opposite side of his pole, repeat the move. Continue, making each upward squeeze last at least ten seconds. After every fifth upward squeeze, throw in a quick, firm, up-and-down pump stroke.

25

When in doubt, press even harder. What would make you writhe in pain will make him writhe with delight because his skin tends to be tougher and thicker than yours. If you're not sure how hard, have him give you a hands-on demo of how he likes to touch himself, and then follow his lead.

26

Once you have the basics down cold, throw these make-his-toes-curl handholds into the mix.

- **The Tickler:** Make his Mr Happy even happier by lightly tracing your fingers over the entire area.
- **The Big Squeeze:** Press your palms flat against the sides of the shaft and press hard while moving your hands up and down.
- **The Corkscrew:** Squeeze the head of his penis and gently wiggle it back and forth while holding the base with your other hand.
- **The Kneader:** Hold his baguette so that your thumbs are touching. Lightly pull in opposite directions and then come back together.
- **The Ring:** Encircle just below the head of his penis with your thumb and forefinger and pump up and down with it.

27

Do any of the above in public and he will worship at your feet.

Flicking Him Off

Easier than patting your head while rubbing your belly, using your hands and mouth on him at the same time will make him feel like he has the starring role in a ménage à trois.

With your mouth around his penis, tickle his balls with one hand using your other hand to scratch his inner thighs or stroke his bottom.

28

Prick his prick. According to acupuncture, there are meridians – interconnected channels of energy – running through the body. To get in touch with his amorous avenue, pop him into your mouth while pressing the base of his big toe with the heel of your hand. Follow-up with a rub along the top of his foot and up the inside of his leg. When you get to his inner thighs, slow down and lighten your pressure to fingertips only while you trace around his testicles and his tummy, ending up on his chest.

29

30

Sometimes a subtle unexpected pressure makes the difference between a fan-sucking-tastic session and a blah one. Here are three jabs he wants you to give him.

- Use your thumbs to press lightly on the sides of his shaft while your tongue does the talking.
- Squish hard against his perineum with your thumb, moving it in tiny circles.
- If you're game and he's down, put your (well-moistened) pointer in his rear (slowly, gently!).

31

Give his hot rod a rub 'n' shine. Tightly grasp
his shaft in your hand just below the glans and
slightly twist while using the flat of your tongue
to swirl just around the rim of the head.

Use one hand to guide
his penis into your mouth,
and then, looking him
in the eye, reach up with
both hands to tweak
his nipples.

33

Squirt
stingily;
being too
generous removes
friction (what his penis
thrives on). Squeeze one drop on
the palm of your hand and one on
the tip of his rod and get steamy.
Uncut Version: You probably
won't need much lube since the
ultrasensitive skin is covered
by the foreskin.

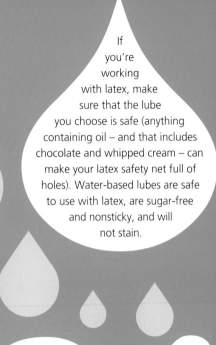

If you're working with latex, make sure that the lube you choose is safe (anything containing oil – and that includes chocolate and whipped cream – can make your latex safety net full of holes). Water-based lubes are safe to use with latex, are sugar-free and nonsticky, and will not stain.

34

35

Merge two favourite hobbies – eating and sex – with yummy-flavoured lubes. There are chocolate creams to satisfy your sweet tooth, champagne and strawberry dick lick drops and fruity oils if you don't like your treats artificially flavoured. Check out the lube selection at sex shops such as www.blowfish.com and www.annsummers.com.

36

Make like a wild scientist and sexperiment. Some lubes list glycerine or cinnamon, peppermint or clove oils in the ingredients. When you smear these on his skin and blow, his hotdog will heat up to boiling point. Others contain benzocaine or other mild anaesthetics that numb the skin and trigger an amazing sensation when they wear off. (Heads up: The deadening action means you may also be sucking on his lollipop for a long, long time.) Check out tip 34 before using.

37

Want to feel like a natural woman?
Then drizzle him with Bodywise
Liquid Silk or Astroglide, lubes which
most closely mimic your own natural
body secretions (see tip 35 for
information on where to buy).

Accept no substitutions. Do-it-yourself lubes such as deodorant, hair gel, body lotion and petroleum jelly can cause chemical burns on his most sensitive bits. Follow this rule of thumb: If it's safe to eat, it's probably safe to smear on his dick (honey, ice cream, butter, yogurt, syrup and cheese spread are a few buffet examples – but skip anything spicy like salsa or mustard). Check tip 34 for protection issues.

33

Propping Him Up

Send the amorous action to new heights by adding a few toys to your oral play (see tip 35 for shop-til-you-drop sources).

Get a buzz on the next time you dive between his legs.

- Use a finger vibrator on his balls, perineum and rear hole.
- Slide a slimline vibrator behind his balls.
- Rest your chin on top of a wand vibrator.
- Hold a small vibrator against your cheek.

39

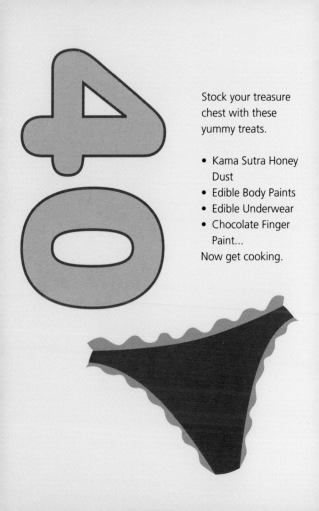

Stock your treasure chest with these yummy treats.

- Kama Sutra Honey Dust
- Edible Body Paints
- Edible Underwear
- Chocolate Finger Paint...

Now get cooking.

41

Want to express your inner erotic artiste? Dip a soft-bristled paintbrush in frosting or chocolate syrup and use his groin as your canvas. Then devour your masterpiece.

42

Wrap a silk scarf or a strand of love beads around your hand and slide it up and down the shaft and head of his penis.

Section Three

Lucky Stiff

Variety's always welcome in the land down under (unless it involves sharp objects). The trick lies in knowing how to branch out from your basic slide-lick-suck and work his other bits into the action in a way that is most likely to make him your love slave. Hint: It's all about the build-up. Too much too soon and he could end up losing his concentration while too little too late and you could end up down there until the next millennium. So start small and finish big. Be warned: Perfect these beg-for-mercy manoeuvres and he may never want to get out of bed!

Ball Play

It's time to play with the family jewels.

43

Put both his balls in your mouth at once. Use one hand to circle the top of the sac and gently pull down to bring the balls together into a neat easy-to-swallow package. Then gently suck, hum a little tune and twirl with your tongue.

44

As you give his wicket your oral best, reach up and gently pull on his balls, working your hands in tandem with your mouth moves to virtually double the sensation.

45

Squeeze his sack as he peaks. Just before ejaculation, his testicles will rise like a pair of hot-air balloons to provide more power to his orgasmic trip into the stratosphere. Adding pressure will turbocharge his blast-off.

46

Feverishly flicking your tongue along his raphe (the vertical line in the middle of his scrotal sac) will send an electric volt through his system.

47

Lightly graze your fingernails over his balls and the crease between his thigh and groin. For the first few seconds, barely touch him. As he gets used to the sensation – and his penis starts straightening up – apply more pressure (never scratching!), running the smooth tops of your nails forward and back. Take care: One misplaced talon could wreak havoc.

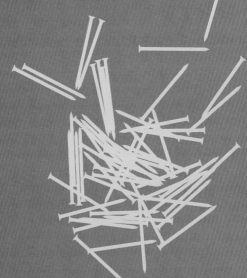

Get In the Zone

Let your mouth roam over the hottest places on and around his penis.

Give his love warrior a tongue lashing it'll never forget. Plant big wet ones over every inch of him. Start by pressing your tongue against the tip of the glans. Then tap it repeatedly against his fraenulum and press it flat against the sides of his hard-on using sweeping strokes as you lick up and down. Do it again... and again. By the third cycle, he'll either be convinced he's died and gone to heaven or he'll have passed out from utter joy.

48

His bottom isn't a black hole to be avoided at all costs. It's actually packed with sensitive nerves just begging for licking. Sweep his backfield with a stiff tongue. If you can't get beyond the bog factor, slip a cut-up condom over the area (the extra material may even boost the sensation). But check out tips 84 to 85 for info on washing behind his ears and tip 86 for the inside track on STIs (sexually transmitted infections) before hitting on his back door.

49

50

Play with his prostate and watch him prostrate himself before you. Hard to reach, this internal walnut-size gland is a pleasure minefield. Wrapping your lips (and hand, if necessary) around the shaft of his penis and, rather than doing your usual up-and-down thing, moving it toward his body will treat him to an inner massage.

To knead him into orgasmic oblivion, work your fingers against his perineum as you mouth him off.

Tongue Twisters

Nine tantalizing tactics that will keep him coming...
back for more.

52

While moving up his shaft
with your mouth, shake
your head from side to side
(as if you're saying no),
letting your tongue follow a
corkscrew pattern. Repeat,
moving down his shaft.

53

Take everything really, really s-l-o-w-l-y.

54

Work out – it will help you hold your breath longer.

55

Give him a hummer. Simply go "mmmm" for a few seconds on the head of his penis. Work your range: A low pitch makes slow vibrations; a higher one speeds things up.

56

Try this Taoist twist: Go shallow for nine bobs, go deep on the tenth. Then repeat the pattern, but this time do eight shallow bobs and two deep ones. Continue until you've worked your way down to one shallow bob and nine incredibly deep ones. Then do the shimmy, shimmy shake and get into his groove.

Do almost-oral sex where you get real close to his swag and then pass by with just a hot breath. Ignore his pleas. After about five of the longest minutes of his life, gobble him up.

57 58

Use your tongue to trace letters on his wee-wee for great initial stimulation. The pointed, firm tongue strokes will have him screaming for you to dot the "I".

59

Melt him faster than ice in a desert with long, slow tongue drags from bottom to top (like licking an ice lolly). Flatten your tongue to get the most surface-to-surface.

While deep-throating won't necessarily boost his pleasure Q (the most sensitive part of his little friend is the head), it will boost his estimation of your oral powers. Here's how to swallow his sword without messing up your lipstick.

- Pay attention to the angle of his dangle – work from above with an up-curving penis and below with a down-pointing one.

- If you gag easily, point him slightly toward the side of your throat instead of straight down. He won't go in as deep but he'll never notice the difference.

- Stop and relax your throat muscles every ½ in (1.3 cm) or so before letting him go deeper.

- Swallow – when his wand tickles the back your throat, that is. It will help gag your gag reflex and widen things.

On the Side

Here are eight treats you can add to the main menu to make things even more delicious.

61 Men are visually stimulated so give him a feast for his eyes by keeping the lights on so he can see his penis move in and out of your mouth.

62 Give him a wash 'n' dry. First, blow him with your mouth and then blow him with a hairdryer set on low.

63

Apply some bright red lipstick before lipping him off (it double-duties as a great lube).

64

Do him in a car. If possible, a red convertible. Preferably when he is not driving.

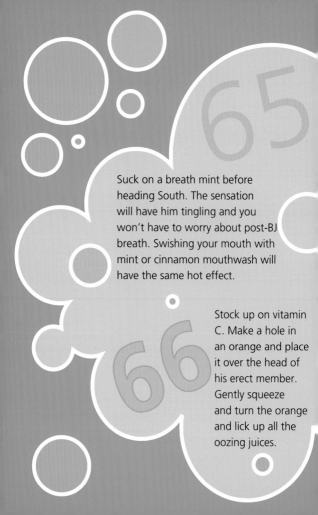

65

Suck on a breath mint before heading South. The sensation will have him tingling and you won't have to worry about post-BJ breath. Swishing your mouth with mint or cinnamon mouthwash will have the same hot effect.

66

Stock up on vitamin C. Make a hole in an orange and place it over the head of his erect member. Gently squeeze and turn the orange and lick up all the oozing juices.

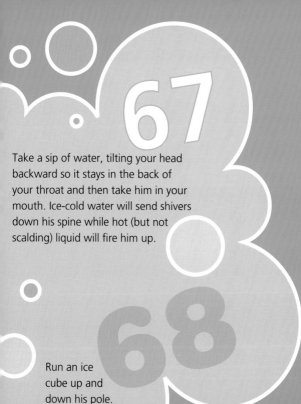

67

Take a sip of water, tilting your head backward so it stays in the back of your throat and then take him in your mouth. Ice-cold water will send shivers down his spine while hot (but not scalding) liquid will fire him up.

68

Run an ice cube up and down his pole.

Section Four

The Big Gulp

Spit or swallow? For most blokes, it's a non-starter. The way they see it, their bodies have been working to produce that brew all day long. It's good stuff. But you may need a few more reasons. Try these on for size.

- Despite appearances, it's only about a teaspoon of semen.
- It's low-calorie and brimming with nutrients.
- The vitamin E content will give your skin a healthy glow.
- Unlike spitting, it's no muss or fuss so you can orally surprise him just about anywhere.

Ready? Here's how to go with his flow.

Blast-off

We've got lift-off. Here's how to prepare so you're not caught with your jaw hanging open.

If his penis swells, his body tenses and his balls draw close to his body, he's gonna blow (shouts of "I'm coooommming" are also a dead give-away). Instantly recall what he does with his body during his intercourse orgasms – does he start jackhammering or does he stay slow and steady? Try mimicking the action with your mouth.

69

70

The second his flares go off,
up the stimulation by pressing
firmly against his perineum.

If you want to bring him around for Round Two when he's already climaxed, caress his ding-dong lightly with your tongue.

71

Cocktail Party

How to swallow without gagging, making faces or saying "yuck".

Want to know what his semen will taste like without swallowing a drop? Check his diet.

- Too much fast food or spicy and salty snacks can give him a pungent zest.
- An overindulgence of booze, coffee and ciggies may lead to a bad taste in your mouth.
- Asparagus, broccoli, onions and garlic add a bitter note to his character.

Bland foods like pasta, fruit and potatoes will keep his taste finger lickin' good. Heads up: If he used to taste differently, he may have an STI such as trichomoniasis or chlamydia. You'll both need to get checked out by a doctor immediately (study up on poison penises in tip 86).

Get a taster. When he's hot to trot, his Cowper's glands (located at the base of his penis) produce a liquid that lubes his urethra so semen can blast through fancy free. This stuff tastes a lot like the real thing and leaks in manageable dribbles just before he ejaculates.

73

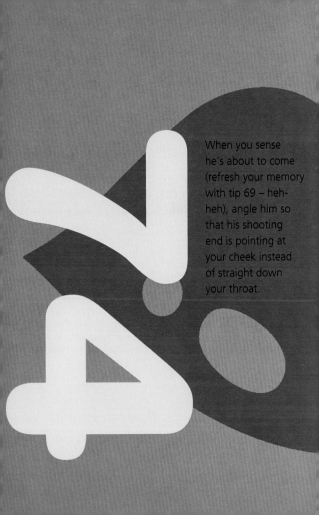

When you sense he's about to come (refresh your memory with tip 69 – heh-heh), angle him so that his shooting end is pointing at your cheek instead of straight down your throat.

75

Dentistry isn't exactly a romantic profession, but a recent study on oral pain and acupressure found that if he puts the first three fingers of his hand together and presses them against the inside of your wrist (aka the P-6 region) while simultaneously poking around your mouth, the gag reflect diminishes considerably.

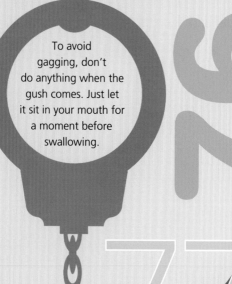

To avoid gagging, don't do anything when the gush comes. Just let it sit in your mouth for a moment before swallowing.

Pretend he's your fantasy of the month.

Clean Finish

Ditch the spit kit. There are lots of things you can do with his semen besides swallowing it.

Give him a dry orgasm. Contrary to popular belief, a man's orgasm and his ejaculation are an inseparable team. A study at the State University of New York Health Science Center at Brooklyn found that men can actually learn to climax three to ten times before ejaculating by flexing their pubococcygeal muscle (the one he uses to control his pee flow).

78

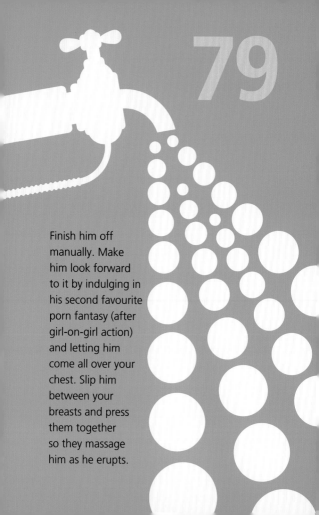

79

Finish him off manually. Make him look forward to it by indulging in his second favourite porn fantasy (after girl-on-girl action) and letting him come all over your chest. Slip him between your breasts and press them together so they massage him as he erupts.

80

If you finish him off by hand, add some water-based lube to give your digits the warmth and wetness of your mouth.

Don't put your mouth out of action completely. You can still lick the general area while you move over to manhandling him. Make sure you have some tissues or a towel nearby to wipe up the spillage.

Switch to intercourse just before the crucial moment.

82

If he catches you off-guard, don't spit back in his face. Instead, let his fluids dribble all over your face.

83

Section Five

BJ
Blunders

Any man lucky enough to be on the receiving
end of your marvellous mouth magic should
show the proper grace and appreciation (or, at the
very least, reciprocation). So, if he pushes your head
down or holds it in a vice-like grip, caution him
with a little tooth action. Also, remind him that
your ears are not handles. And no, do not do
him while he watches the game.

Read on for other ways to help him
mind his manners.

Poison Penises

Hopefully you won't accidentally bump into
any of these snake charmers in the dark.

IT SMELLS FUNKY:

- A dusting of cornstarch will keep stinky sweat from
  festering down there during the day and be gone by
  the time you want to nose around.

- If he has a stinky or sour odour that doesn't disappear
  once he showers, either he needs to adjust his diet
  (does he relish anything in tip 72?) or he has an
  infection (proceed instantly to tip 86) or a smegma
  build-up (see tip 85 below). If it's just the way he tastes,
  check out tip 35 to see how he can sweeten up his act.

IT LOOKS DIRTY:

- If you can't get it out of your head that he pees and
  comes with the same tool, send him to the showers
  before giving him an oral bath...

- Or you can work him into a lather by soaping him
  down yourself.

- **Uncut Version:** Smegma, a cheesy substance, can
  form under the loose flap of skin if he doesn't wash
  behind his little guy's ears. Pull back his foreskin and
  gently wipe.

IT'S TOXIC:

- The average guy has a 60% chance of being infected with a sexually transmitted infection (STI).

- While penile skin is often bumpy (naturally or because he has sebaceous cysts of hair follicles, an allergic reaction or pearly penile papules – all of which are nothing to worry about), it may also mean he has HPV (human papilloma virus or genital warts), MCV (molluscum contagiosum virus), syphilis or herpes – all infections you can catch through skin-to-skin contact.

- HIV, hepatitis B, hepatitis C and cytomegalovirus (CMV) can also be passed orally. And if you have a cold sore, you can pass this infection onto his willy and he may then develop full-blown genital herpes.

- Bottom Line: Until you both get a clean bill of health from a doctor, don't go near his naked penis (look opposite for the lowdown on using a condom).

- If you have even the slightest question about his penis health, dress him up in a condom first. Skip the prelubricated kinds, which tend to have a bad taste and opt for a more lickable one, flavoured like fruit or candy, instead.

- **Uncut Version:** Max out on the sensation he feels when using a condom by making sure the foreskin is completely pulled back before rolling on the rubber.

- If you both have a clean bill of health, perfect the ultimate party trick by slipping him into his rubbers with your mouth (a reversible polyurethane like eZ-on is designed to unfold in either direction, so you don't need to worry about accidentally contaminating the business side). Once he has a little backbone, hold the condom very gently in your mouth with the opening facing out. Take a deep breath to create suction and then, using your tongue to help, gently roll it down your lover's penis with your lips (practice on a banana first).

IT'S HAIRY:

- No one likes to find hair in the meal. He's probably never once thought about below-the-belt hair grooming. But tell him that not only will a trim give you better access to his shaft, it will also make him look bigger – and watch how fast he starts snipping.

- Make his buzz cut part of your erotic play. Use an electric beard clipper or bikini trimmer to add some sweet vibrations.

Speed Him Up

Blowjobs can occasionally be a lot of work (hence the name). If you're at the point where your mind is wandering and wondering whether that cute bag you want to buy went on sale yet, don't throw in the towel. Here are five things guaranteed to send him into happy oblivion in less time than it takes to say, "Are you close to coming?"

88

Work all his bits and pieces at the same time (see tips 28 to 32 for ideas).

89

Drop everything and zone in on his fraenulum. This ultrasensitive area is like a male clitoris – packed with nerve endings, it's a no-fail big-O trigger. With every lick, add a little extra tongue pressure in that one spot until he climaxes.

Wrap your thumb and index finger around the shaft, about 1 in (2.5 cm) above the base, and pull down while sucking down on the head. He'll probably climax in two minutes tops.

Launch sequence still not happening? Give it up and make him come another way – with your hand or via intercourse. Save face by sighing, "You made me so hot I can't wait to feel you inside of me."

92

If your mouth is tired, stick your tongue out as far as you can and press down. Now you can use your neck muscles instead, and you'll be able to stay the course without getting tongue-tied.

Slow Him Down

Of course, if he comes fast it may just mean that you are very, very good. However, it also means he may now roll over and fall into a post-O coma. To slow him down to your climatic time, unashamedly try one (or more) of the following tricks.

93

When you sense that he's reaching his pleasure peak (see tip 69 for clues), stop touching him completely for 30 seconds. That should be enough time for him to get in control of himself.

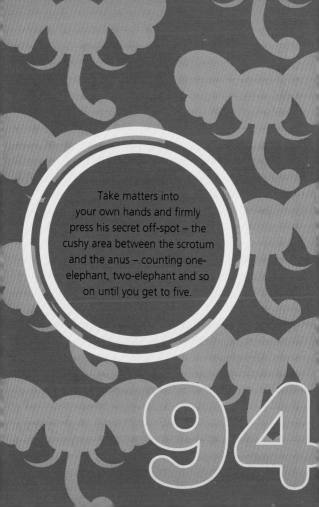

Take matters into
your own hands and firmly
press his secret off-spot – the
cushy area between the scrotum
and the anus – counting one-
elephant, two-elephant and so
on until you get to five.

94

Slip a ring on him. Not a wedding ring (although that may also cool his heels), but a cock ring. It will trap blood in the penis, which means he's yours for as long as you want him (20 minutes is the max to avoid damaging the capillaries and bruising the penis).

Try a style that goes on easily (even after he's hardened up) and can be adjusted and taken off, like a Velcro ring (see tip 35 for resources). The tighter you make it, the more intense the release.

96

Tell him that male participation is required in this event. If he's lying back and doing nothing, casually mention that if he gives you a reason to enjoy going South of his belly border, you'll keep coming back for more.

It Takes Two to Tango

A BJ doesn't have to be a one-way road. Here, for your reading pleasure, are five things he can do to you to while you do him.

Position yourself over him so he has easy access to your bits and pieces – and no excuses. And because you're on top, you can decide when to pause for moans (but don't leave him hanging – continue working him over with your hands).

If his hands on you is too much of a distraction for you to give proper attention to the (blow)job at hand, suggest he redirects his touches. He may not be able to press your love button but he can still play with your hair, stroke your face, run his fingers over your back and knead your shoulders.

98

99

Ask him to
hold your hair back
out of your face (added
incentive – he'll get a
better view of
the action).

100

Remind him there is no such thing as too much flattery. Anything along the lines of "You look so sexy between my legs," "I love and adore you" and "You give the best head I ever received" should guarantee him a second below-the-belt round.